Echoes Of Life And Beyond

Poetry from life's edge to the divine heart

B.M.Jain "RUHAAN"

/ BookLeaf
Publishing

India | USA | UK

Made with ❤ on the BookLeaf Publishing Platform
www.bookleafpub.in
www.bookleafpub.com

Dedication

To the Source of all things —
the Eternal Artist who paints life with light and shadow.
To every soul who has ever stood at the edge of the
unknown,
seeking meaning in silence, and faith in the fire.
And to my family, whose love has been my first prayer
and my constant truth.

Preface

Poetry, to me, is not just expression — it is exploration.
It is where the unseen meets the spoken, where silence finds voice.
The verses in this book were not written in search of answers,
but in devotion to the questions — about life, about love, about the One who made us all.
This book is a reflection of my journey inward and outward, a conversation with life as I see it, feel it, and sometimes, fear it. In moments of joy, doubt, despair, and awe, I found these words flowing — as if from somewhere beyond me. They speak of human ties, of sacred mysteries, of the fragile and the eternal.
 I invite you, the reader, to walk with me — not to agree or disagree —
but to feel, to question, and perhaps, to remember something you had forgotten. If even one poem in these pages echoes your inner voice,
then this book has served its purpose.

 With humility and hope,

[B. M. JAIN "RUHAAN"]

Acknowledgements

With heartfelt gratitude, I bow to the Divine, whose grace has been the true inspiration behind every word of this collection.

I express my deepest thanks to my family, whose love, patience, and encouragement have given me strength at every step of this creative journey. Their faith in me has been the foundation upon which this book stands.

My sincere appreciation goes to my friends and well-wishers, who offered their support, guidance, and kind words that motivated me to keep writing.

I also wish to acknowledge my readers—present and future—because without their hearts to receive these poems, this work would remain incomplete.

Finally, I dedicate this book to all seekers of truth, beauty, and meaning in life. May these poems touch your soul as profoundly as they have touched mine while writing them.

1. 🌹 O' Mother - A big Salute to You 🌹

You wrote the proof of my first breath,
I wrote the script of your silent death.

You heard my very first tender cry,
I heard the whisper of your last goodbye.

You clothed me gently in garments new,
I wrapped you softly in your final hue.

You saved me from storms, from fear and flame,
I laid you to rest in fire's solemn name.

You gave me shade beneath the burning sun,
A quilt in the cold, in summer a breeze to run.

In your boundless love I grew so tall,
But your farewell broke my spirit's wall.

You smiled each dawn when I came in sight,
Now I weep at your photo deep in the night.

O Mother—your debt I can never repay,
In your memory I bow, day after day.

You gifted me life, pure and true,
I gave my last salute to you.

2. 🌹 Woman_ God's Marvelous Creation 🌹

One day a thought the Creator knew,
To shape a form both pure and true.
A marvel rare, the world to see,
A masterpiece of mystery.

From flowers came her tender grace,
From thorns, a sting none could erase.
From dewdrops, soft caress was drawn,
From gardens, fragrance at the dawn.

From mountains, strength so firm, so high,
From earth, her patience deep and shy.
From trees, the gift of sacrifice,
From feelings—warmth and depth precise.

From bubbles, fleeting time He took,
From whirlpools, depth like open book.

From struggles came a sweetness rare,
From ocean waves, her restless care.

From swans, the power of gentle love,
From birds, the flight to rise above.
From crows, the wit that never fails,
From doves, the peace that so prevails.

From ants, the will to toil and strive,
From bees, the zeal to keep alive.
From water, purity refined,
From fire, detachment well-designed.

Thus elements five He did combine,
In sacred art, through thought divine.
At last creation stood begun,
The crowning wonder—woman!

3. 🌹 When God Created Man... 🌹

When God created man one day,
Even heaven smiled in gentle sway.
He thought—"The earth shall need a flame,
To guide through darkness, none the same."

From mighty mountains, courage came,
From saints, pure wisdom lit its flame.
From mothers' hearts, love deep and true,
From banyan shade, calm patience grew.

From battlefields, He drew up might,
From sages' lives, the gift of light.
From Gita's word, the call of duty,
From cows, the grace of gentle beauty.

From Dharma's throne, the sense of right,
From teachers' hands, respect so bright.
From children's smiles, the joy of play,
From Shiva's penance, the steadfast way.

To eyes, He gave far-seeing view,
To hands, the power of work to do.
To heart, compassion vast and kind,
To speech, the truth with nectar lined.

And then the Lord, with smiling face,
Declared with love, His holy grace:
"This man I send to guard the land,
To honor, nurture, and withstand.

O Man! You are not flesh alone,
But purpose deep, by heaven shown.
You are strength, devotion, sacrifice—
The earth's divine and priceless prize."

4. 🌹 Bonding – An Art and a Devotion 🌹

To form a bond is easy to do, like stringing pearls in line,
A smile, a word, a moment shared – and hearts begin to shine.

But to sustain, now that's the path where true devotion lies,
With love, with patience, selfless care — the soul of every tie.

When storms of ego cloud the skies, hold tighter to the thread,
For only trust can build the base where stories may be spread.

The garden of relations blooms when watered well with grace,
Else doubts and distance, lies and hurt, will make it lose its place.

So know — to bond is but an art, a gesture from the start,
But keeping it is sacred work — the worship of the
heart.

5. 🌹 A Smile Amidst the Thorns 🌹

The rose blooms bright amidst the thorns,
Spreading beauty, though it's worn.
It never stops, it never bends,
Through every pain, its fragrance sends.

Its petals softly seem to say,
Joy and sorrow both will stay.
He who fears not thorn or strife,
Finds the truest hues of life.

Life too is such a blooming field,
With trials and truths yet to be revealed.
But one who smiles in storm and rain,
Lights a lamp in dark terrain.

Fall and rise that's how we grow,
Learn to walk where harsh winds blow.
Let your lips wear hope's own art,
Make each moment a work of heart.

This truth life whispers every day,
He who smiles through the hardest way,
Walks the path from soul to divine,
In every thorn, he learns to shine.

6. 🌹 The Lamp Walks Ahead of Us 🌹

When we step into the dark of night,
We believe the lamp guides our sight.
The flame we hold, so calm and bright,
We think it shows the path so right.

But truth lies deeper than it seems,
The lamp walks first, not in our dreams.
We merely follow where it leads,
Its light fulfills our silent needs.

We're not the doers, nor the wise,
Nor makers of the path we prize.
The flame that burns without a sound,
Is inner strength, so deep, profound.

Its glow is not just outwardly,
It ends the dark inside of me.
When pride and ego start to fall,
The soul awakens to the call.

We do not walk — we're led instead,
By sacred light our hearts are fed.
And when divine inspiration flows,
The journey smoothens as it goes.

To that silent flame that never demands,
Yet lights our way with unseen hands.

7. 🌹 Surrender Your Worries to the Universe 🌹

When shadows of doubt begin to rise,
And fear paints clouds across your skies,
When restless nights steal peace away,
And heavy thoughts refuse to sway—

Remember this truth, so simple, so pure,
The Universe holds a healing cure.
Lay down your burdens, release the weight,
Trust in its timing, trust in your fate.

Worry is chains that pull you low,
Faith is the light that helps you grow.
The cosmic embrace is vast, supreme,
Where pain dissolves like a fading dream.

Life unfolds in the now you see,
The future is just a mystery.
What must arrive will find its way,
And dawn will always follow grey.

So breathe in deep, let courage flow,
Smile at the fears you used to know.
And softly whisper, calm and true—

"Dear Universe,

I give this to you."

8. 🌹 The Rare Ones Come by Fate 🌹

Some friends are dearer than the breath we take,
Who love from the heart, not for gifting's sake.

They stand by you when your world's in pain,
Unmoved by fortune, unmoved by gain.

Such bonds aren't sold in any store,
Don't weigh them down with price or score.

They come by fate, these priceless ties,
Who give you their all, with no disguise.

So guard them deep in your heart's own space,
Without them, jewels lose all their grace.

While the world runs after the glittering spree,
True ones arrive by destiny — by God's decree.

9. 🌹 " The Chariot of Life"

The body's a chariot, strong and wide,
The soul is the one who sits inside.
The senses are horses, fast and free,
They run where the mind lets them be.
The mind is the rein, the guide so tight,
The intellect shows what's wrong or right.
If senses go wild and pull apart,
The chariot falls and breaks the heart.
But if the soul is calm and wise,
It sees the truth beyond the lies.
Not just the body, flesh, and skin,
The light within is where we begin.
Control the mind, let wisdom steer,
The path of peace will then be clear.
The soul must lead, not stray or sleep,
For life is a road, both high and deep.
So take the reins, be still, be bright,
                              And let your
soul guide you to light.

10. 🌹 " Company and Character" 🌹

Not every flower is a rose so fair,
Not every tree perfumes the air.
Beauty and grace are seldom found,
In every soul or piece of ground.
Only when saints we choose to near,
The heart turns calm, the mind sincere.
Without their touch, our thoughts decay,
And virtues slowly drift away.
The fruit we bear is not by chance,
But through life's sacred, steadfast dance.
With roots in values, firm and deep,
It's faith and duty that we reap.
Each day the soul is gently fed,
By drops of truth, by what we've read.
A garden grows where goodness flows,
And fragrant blooms of wisdom show.
So walk the path where sages tread,
Let virtues in your heart be spread.
With character your guide and light,

You'll find your
soul both pure and bright.

11. 🌹 The Whisper of the Shore 🌹

Step softly now, as you leave the boat,
The shore awaits—its truths afloat.
Life slides by in a silent stream,
Teaching the depth behind each dream.

No storm appears to stir the tide,
No tether snaps, yet fears may hide .
The shoreline whispers, time and again,
"The journey's long—beyond this plain."

So tread with care, let the mind be still,
Sip each moment, let it fill.
Life too flows, with quiet grace,
Drifting from shores, toward a bolder place.

Unload your boat—but do it slow,
There's wisdom in the softness, though.
Each gentle wave, each breath, each scar,

Shapes who you are—and who you are.

For hidden deep in every glide,
Are truths we carry, not just ride.
And in the hush where waters kiss—
Lives the vastness... of life's abyss.

12. 🌹 The Mystery of Sleep and the Soul 🌹

~~~❦~~~

When twilight whispers, and silence is deep,
The body lies still, yet the soul does not sleep.
Eyes may close, but a door swings wide,
To realms unseen, where the spirits glide.

Dreams are the lanterns, faint and rare,
Glimpses of journeys our soul may share.
Are they but echoes of mind's own streams?
Or windows that open to higher dreams?

In deepest slumber, so calm, so profound,
The self is lost, no "I" is found.
A drop returns to the ocean's shore,
The soul meets the Source it longed for.

Science explains with reasons and schemes,
Chemicals, neurons, and fleeting dreams.
Yet saints have said, in their mystic role—
Sleep is the mirror reflecting the Soul.

So every night, when we drift away,
We practice a truth for the final day:
That life is a dream, and rest makes us whole,
And death is but sleep... for the wandering soul.

13. 🌹 Two Golden Rules for a Peaceful Life 🌹

When failure knocks, don't start to cry,
Let not its shadow reach your sky.
Keep pain outside your gentle heart,
Don't let it tear your soul apart.

These paths are here to teach, to mold,
To help you stand, be brave and bold.
Failure is not the end of road,
But steps to rise and shed your load.

And when success begins to shine,
Don't think yourself some gift divine.
Don't let it rise into your head,
Or pride will grow and truth be dead.

For those who bow are truly tall,
And humbleness outshines them all.
In grace and silence lives real pride,
Not in the roar of swollen tide.

Don't let your heart grow weak with pain,
Nor let your mind with pride be vain.
These two rules, if you live by true,
Will bring you peace in all you do.

14. 🌹 The Essence of Staying Rooted 🌹

A tree stands tall, its roots held tight,
They feed its soul, they grant it light.

When values guide and virtues stay,
Peace and joy will crown each day.

The elders' shade, both deep and wide,
Holds lessons carved by time's harsh tide.

With patient hearts and tranquil grace,
They spread cool comfort in every place.

Cut from its roots, the tree will die,
Its leaves will fade, its branches dry.

So too the soul, if torn apart,
It shines outside, yet starves at heart.

Stay with your roots, let truth be near,
Their strength will guide, their light be clear.

Life blooms with fruit, serene and bright,
When soul unites with God's pure light.

15. 🌹 The Cycle of Life 🌹

In childhood's dawn, there's time to spare,
And strength abounds, beyond compare.
But money's missing, dreams still bloom,
In laughter's light, there's no gloom.

Then youth arrives with power and gold,
Ambitions fierce, and visions bold.
Yet time slips by — it's never near,
The clock keeps running, year by year.

Old age then whispers, calm and slow,
Time returns, and wealth may flow.
But fading strength, the body's plea,
Turns memories to company.

Such is nature's wondrous plan,
No stage completes the perfect span.
So live each day in joy's embrace,
With peace and smiles to fill your space.

For time, for strength, for gold — all three,
Are gifts that come, not all agree.
Today's the treasure, pure and bright,
Live now, with love, in gentle light.

16. 🌹 Beyond the House of Worry 🌹

In the house of worry, peace finds no door,
Joy stands waiting, but enters no more.
Before you chase pleasure, seek calm within,
For where peace dwells, true joy begins.

Happiness alone may fade away,
But peace of mind will choose to stay.
Lay down the burden of anxious thought,
And live the joy your soul has sought.

Worry steals health, it dims life's grace,
So seek bright hope in every place.
Accept what destiny softly weaves,
For nothing arrives before fate believes.

Let peace be your path, and calm your light.

17. 🌹 The Worth of Wisdom and Friendship 🌹

In life's long journey, remember two things true,
Keep wisdom close — it will always guide you.
Never befriend a fool, nor fool a friend,
For both will lead to a bitter end.

A fool knows not the meaning of care,
He mocks your truth, unaware.
Where wisdom fades, peace cannot stay,
So walk with light, and find your way.

And those true friends who stand by your side,
Honor their hearts, in them confide.
For friendship's bond is sacred and deep,
It's trust we sow, and joy we reap.

A true friend shines in the darkest hour,
A silent strength, a soothing power.
Stay away from folly, hold truth near,
Keep friendship pure, both strong and clear.

❧ *Avoid the foolish, be faithful to friends — that's the wisdom life commends.*

18. 🌹 The Flow of Time – All Shall Stay on Earth 🌹

~~~⚜~~~

I've seen the world change colors each passing day,
And watched life itself find new patterns, new way.
Those who once strode with a lion's pride,
Now seek a hand to walk beside.

Eyes that once could make the strong men shake,
Now weep like clouds in the monsoon's ache.
Hands that shattered stone with a gentle sign,
Now tremble like leaves on a fragile line.

Voices that thundered like lightning's might,
Now locked in silence, lost their light.
Youth, strength, and wealth — all gifts divine,
Yet I've seen souls empty, despite their shine.

So, my friend, don't boast of your today,
Time's river humbles all on its way.
If you can — bring joy to someone's heart,
For I've seen countless who tore lives apart.

Because in the end —
No fame, no fortune, no ego shall stay,
All that belongs to this earth...
Shall rest upon this clay.

19. 🌹 Endurance – The True Strength of Life 🌹

<hr/>

Sorrows haven't grown in this world, my friend,
It's patience that's begun to bend.
The storms aren't stronger than before —
It's hearts that break a little more.

Once, pain could melt into a smile,
Now tears flow for things so mild.
When endurance fades, the mind turns weak,
Peace departs, and chaos we seek.

But the one who learns the art to bear,
Finds calmness blooming everywhere.
He smiles amid the wildest storm,
For patience keeps his spirit warm.

It's easy to drown — to be the sea,
But rare to be the stream that sets one free.
Be not the wave that pulls below,

Be the hand that helps hearts grow.

So learn to bear, to stand, to stay,
Find pearls in trials along your way.
For endurance is that sacred art,
That makes divine the human heart.

Because —
"Those who endure, remain and rise,
Those who escape, their spirit dies."

In patience lies the quiet secret of lasting joy.

20. 🌹 Trust in Divine Timing 🌹

~~~~~~~~~~

What is meant for you will surely come,
Have patience, let the heart be calm.
Do your deeds and let go of gain,
Trust the Divine — beyond joy and pain.

Each seed sleeps in its destined hour,
Each flower waits to reveal its power.
Every wave knows where to flow,
In surrender, its direction grows.

Rush not, nor fear delay,
The Lord's rhythm never goes astray.
He knows when to give and when to withhold,
When to soften, and when to mold.

The moon wanes only to shine again,
The darkest night births dawn's refrain.
So flows life, both still and deep,
Faith is the vow the soul must keep.

Breathe in peace, release your will,
Let silent trust your being fill.
The time will come, divinely true —
When the soul surrenders, and God meets you.

21. 🌹 Dialogue with the Universe 🌹

Cleanse your mind, keep your heart pure,
Connect with the cosmos — your path will be sure.
What you believe in with faith so true,
The universe listens, and brings it to you.

The sky's not distant, it dwells inside,
An endless ocean, vast and wide.
When your vibrations with its rhythm align,
Desires transform, with a touch divine.

Ask with a heart that is humble and clear,
The universe answers, it draws you near.
Keep the flame of patience and trust alive,
All that you seek, in time will arrive.

Simple the secret, profound the plan,
Direct link with the cosmos — the wisdom of man.